ABT

U.S. WARS

WORLD WAR II
IN THE PACIFIC

A MyReportLinks.com Book

R. Conrad Stein

MyReportLinks.com Books
an imprint of
 Enslow Publishers, Inc. E
Box 398, 40 Industrial Road
Berkeley Heights, NJ 07922
USA

MyReportLinks.com Books, an imprint of Enslow Publishers, Inc.

Library of Congress Cataloging-in-Publication Data

Stein, R. Conrad.
    World War II in the Pacific / R. Conrad Stein.
      p. cm. — (U.S. wars)
    Summary: Examines the action in the Pacific theater of World War II,
focusing on the confrontation between the United States and Japan.
Includes Internet links to Web sites, source documents, and photographs
related to the war.
      Includes bibliographical references and index.
      ISBN 0-7660-5093-9
      1. World War, 1939–1945—Campaigns—Pacific Area—Juvenile literature.
2. World War, 1939–1945—United States—Juvenile literature. [1. World
War, 1939–1945—Campaigns—Pacific Area. 2. World War, 1939–1945—United
States.] I. Title: World War Two in the Pacific. II. Title: World War 2 in the Pacific. III. Title. IV. Series.
    D767 .S75 2002
    940.54'26—dc21
                    2001008211

Printed in the United States of America

10 9 8 7 6 5 4 3 2 1

To Our Readers:
Through the purchase of this book, you and your library gain access to the Report Links that specifically
back up this book.
The Publisher will provide access to the Report Links that back up this book and will keep these Report
Links up to date on **www.myreportlinks.com** for three years from the book's first publication date.
We have done our best to make sure all Internet addresses in this book were active and appropriate when we
went to press. However, the author and the Publisher have no control over, and assume no liability for, the
material available on those Internet sites or on other Web sites they may link to.
The usage of the MyReportLinks.com Books Web site is subject to the terms and conditions stated on the
Usage Policy Statement on **www.myreportlinks.com**.
In the future, a password may be required to access the Report Links that back up this book. The password
is found on the bottom of page 4 of this book.
Any comments or suggestions can be sent by e-mail to comments@myreportlinks.com or to the address on
the back cover.

Photo Credits: © Corel Corporation, pp. 1 (background), 3; Courtesy of Children of the Camps,
pp. 25, 26; Courtesy of IwoJima.com, p. 35; Courtesy of MyReportLinks.com Books, p. 4; Courtesy
of New York Times on the Web, p. 43; Courtesy of The American Experience/PBS, p. 33; Courtesy of
The History Place, p. 18; Courtesy of The Pacific War: The U.S. Navy, p. 20; Courtesy of National Air
and Space Museum, p. 41; Enslow Publishers, pp. 27, 31; Library of Congress, pp. 13, 15, 22, 30, 38,
39; National Archives, pp. 1, 12, 17, 36, 42.

Cover Photo: AP/Wide World Photos

Cover Description: The USS *West Virginia*, sunk during the attack on Pearl Harbor, December
7, 1941.

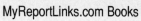
Contents

MyReportLinks.com Books
Great Books, Great Links, Great for Research!

MyReportLinks.com Books present the information you need to learn about your report subject. In addition, they show you where to go on the Internet for more information. The pre-evaluated Report Links that back up this book are kept up to date on **www.myreportlinks.com**. With the purchase of a MyReportLinks.com Books title, you and your library gain access to the Report Links that specifically back up that book. The Report Links save hours of research time and link to dozens—even hundreds—of Web sites, source documents, and photos related to your report topic.

Please see "To Our Readers" on the Copyright page for important information about this book, the MyReportLinks.com Books Web site, and the Report Links that back up this book.

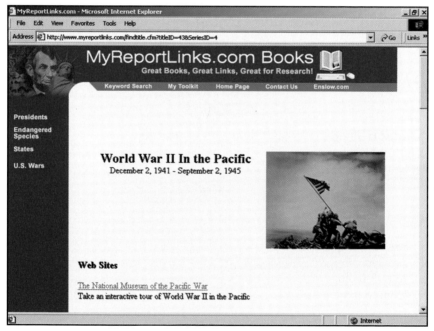

Access:

The Publisher will provide access to the Report Links that back up this book and will try to keep these Report Links up to date on our Web site for three years from the book's first publication date. Please enter **UWP9296** if asked for a password.

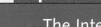

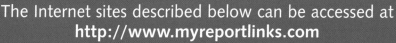

The Internet sites described below can be accessed at
http://www.myreportlinks.com

▶**The National Museum of the Pacific War**   *Editor's choice*
At this Web site you can take an interactive tour of World War II in the
Pacific. The tour provides an overview of major battles and causes of
the war from 1941 to 1945.

Link to this Internet site from http://www.myreportlinks.com
Editor's choice
▶**The American Experience: MacArthur**
This informative Web site provides information about General
MacArthur's military career and his role in World War II in the Pacific.
You will also find links to interactive maps and a time line.

Link to this Internet site from http://www.myreportlinks.com
Editor's choice
▶**National Geographic: Remembering Pearl Harbor**
An excellent site about Pearl Harbor includes a multimedia map, time
line, biographies, and historical information.

Link to this Internet site from http://www.myreportlinks.com
Editor's choice
▶**The Avalon Project: World War II Documents**
This site contains transcriptions of World War II war documents,
including the United States declaration of war against Japan, Germany,
and Italy, as well as Japan's surrender documents.

Link to this Internet site from http://www.myreportlinks.com
Editor's choice
▶**Race for the Superbomb**
At this site you can learn about the race for the superbomb. Here you
can explore time lines, maps, and the people involved in the race for
the superbomb. You will also find video footage of blast tests.

Link to this Internet site from http://www.myreportlinks.com
Editor's choice
▶**Rabbit in the Moon**
This Web site companion to the documentary *Rabbit in the Moon*,
explores the feelings of Japanese Americans held in internment camps
during World War II. Each section of the Web site provides different
points of view and experiences had by Japanese Americans.
Link to this Internet site from http://www.myreportlinks.com

Report Links

The Internet sites described below can be accessed at
http://www.myreportlinks.com

▶ **Air Raid on Pearl Harbor**
This is a comprehensive site that includes photographs of Pearl Harbor, the original radiogram reporting the attack, President Roosevelt's address to Congress, and a link to the "Day of Infamy" speech.

Link to this Internet site from http://www.myreportlinks.com

▶ **Atomic Bomb: Decision**
This site is all about the decision to drop the atomic bomb on Japan. It contains links to military documents, transcripts of Truman's writings and speeches, and petitions by some who were against using the bomb.

Link to this Internet site from http://www.myreportlinks.com

▶ **Children of the Camps: The Documentary**
This Web site companion to the documentary *Children of the Camps*, explores the physical and psychological trauma Japanese-American children experienced from being imprisoned in internment camps during World War II.

Link to this Internet site from http://www.myreportlinks.com

▶ ***Conscience* and the *Constitution***
This Web site companion to the documentary *Conscience* and *Constitution* provides a history of Japanese Americans held in internment camps who refused to go to war while imprisoned in the camps.

Link to this Internet site from http://www.myreportlinks.com

▶ ***Enola Gay***
This Web site contains information about the restoration and history of *Enola Gay*. Here you will learn about the crew and the evolution of *Enola Gay*. You will also find additional information about Boeing B-29s.

Link to this Internet site from http://www.myreportlinks.com

▶ **Iwo Jima**
This site offers information about the Battle of Iwo Jima, including the location of the island, the Japanese strategy, and United States invasion.

Link to this Internet site from http://www.myreportlinks.com

Report Links

The Internet sites described below can be accessed at
http://www.myreportlinks.com

▶ **The Japanese American Internment**
An information filled site containing quotes, memories of
internment victims, original posters from this era, time lines, and
maps of the camps.

Link to this Internet site from http://www.myreportlinks.com

▶ **Japan Surrenders, Ends of War!**
At the *New York Times* Learning Network you will find the front
page article from August 14, 1945, that reported the end of the war
with Japan.

Link to this Internet site from http://www.myreportlinks.com

▶ **Japanese Surrender Okinawa**
At this site you will learn about the day Japanese troops surrendered
Okinawa to the United States. You will also find links to other World
War II resources.

Link to this Internet site from http://www.myreportlinks.com

▶ **National Museum of Naval Aviation**
At this Web site you can explore the history of naval aviation. Some
exhibits featured at this Web site are the Flying Tigers, the Home Front
USA, and the Underwater exhibit.

Link to this Internet site from http://www.myreportlinks.com

▶ **National Museum of the Pacific War**
This National Museum of the Pacific War Web site contains
descriptions and pictures of artifacts from the Pacific War, and a
gallery dedicated to George Bush and his service in the war.

Link to this Internet site from http://www.myreportlinks.com

▶ **The Official Web site of Brig Gen Paul W. Tibbets**
This Web site, dedicated to Brigadier General Paul W. Tibbets, explores
the evolution of the *Enola Gay*, the decision to drop the bomb,
and the event itself. You will also find a collection of photos and
additional links.

Link to this Internet site from http://www.myreportlinks.com

The Internet sites described below can be accessed at
http://www.myreportlinks.com

▶ **The Pacific War: The U.S. Navy**
An informative Web site containing specifics about battles, ships, statistics, pictorials, and personal experiences during the Pacific War.

Link to this Internet site from http://www.myreportlinks.com

▶ **Rosie the Riveter Trust**
An interesting site devoted to the memorial of "Rosie the Riveter." Here you will learn about women who participated in the war effort by working industrial jobs during World War II. This site also contains information about the female labor force in Richmond, California.

Link to this Internet site from http://www.myreportlinks.com

▶ **Submarines in the Pacific War**
This brief site contains statistics regarding submarines used in the Pacific War, and lists their evolution of design and strategies.

Link to this Internet site from http://www.myreportlinks.com

▶ **Truman: Chronology 1945–1949**
President Truman ordered the bombing of Hiroshima in Japan, which ended World War II. At this Web site you will find a time line of Harry Truman's presidential activities and involvement with Japan during World War II.

Link to this Internet site from http://www.myreportlinks.com

▶ **A Veteran's Story: World War II**
This site contains profiles of World War II veterans, along with their photographs. Pilots, naval officers, nurses, and others recount their experiences during the war.

Link to this Internet site from http://www.myreportlinks.com

▶ **Wars and Conflict: World War II**
This is an interesting site that contains some pages about Japan's turning against the West in the early Twentieth century. There is also some information about kamikaze pilots.

Link to this Internet site from http://www.myreportlinks.com

Report Links

The Internet sites described below can be accessed at
http://www.myreportlinks.com

▶**War Relocation Authority Camps in Arizona, 1942–1946**
At this Web site you will find information about Arizona's two
internment camps. Included are maps and pictures.

Link to this Internet site from http://www.myreportlinks.com

▶**World War II Aviation**
At this site you can learn about the many different aircraft used in
World World II.

Link to this Internet site from http://www.myreportlinks.com

▶**World War II Commemoration**
This site has lots of information about the war in the Pacific, and
focuses on the incidents leading up to Japan's quest for power.

Link to this Internet site from http://www.myreportlinks.com

▶**A World War II Diary in the Pacific**
This interesting site contains the concise diary of Jack McKnight,
which lists his daily activities as a seaman aboard the USS *Essex*.

Link to this Internet site from http://www.myreportlinks.com

▶**World War II in the Pacific**
At this Web site you can explore maps detailing operations and planned
actions of American and Japanese forces during World War II under
General Douglas MacArthur.

Link to this Internet site from http://www.myreportlinks.com

▶**World War II in the Pacific: Timeline of
events 1941–1945**
This site lists important events that took place in the Pacific War from
1941–1945. Exact dates of battles and invasions are given.

Link to this Internet site from http://www.myreportlinks.com

▶ Combatants

Allies: United States; Great Britain; France; the Soviet Union; China; Australia; Canada; Italy (after Sept. 8, 1943) and others.

Axis: Japan; Germany; Italy (before Sept. 8, 1943); and others.

Casualties*	Killed	Wounded
United States	291,557	670,846
Soviet Union	6,115,000	14,012,000
China	1,324,516	1,762,006
Japan	1,270,000	140,000

*Casualty totals reflect all military losses by participants in the Pacific War, including battles fought in Europe, Africa, and Asia.

▶ Time Line of the Pacific War

1941—*Dec. 7:* Japanese airplanes bomb Pearl Harbor, Hawaii, thereby igniting war in the Pacific.

—*Dec. 8:* United States Congress declares war on Japan.

—*Late Dec.* to *April 1942:* Japan conquers Singapore, the Philippines, Guam, and Wake Island; the nation reaches the zenith of its power in the Pacific.

1942—*Feb. 19:* President Roosevelt signs Executive Order 9066, which forces Americans of Japanese heritage to move away from their homes on the western coast of the United States.

—*April 18:* American bombers make a daring raid on Japan.

—*May 4* to *May 8:* The Battle of the Coral Sea.

—*June 3* to *June 6:* The Battle of Midway.

—*Aug. 7:* Marines invade the island of Guadalcanal.

1943—*Nov. 20:* Marines land on Tarawa.

1944—*Oct. 20:* Army troops land on Leyte and begin the reconquest of the Philippines.

1945—*Feb. 19:* U.S. Marines invaded the island of Iwo Jima.

—*April 1:* Marine and army units assault Okinawa.

—*July 16:* The first atomic bomb is test fired.

—*Aug. 6:* An atomic bomb is dropped on Hiroshima, Japan.

—*Aug. 9:* A second atomic bomb is dropped on Nagasaki, Japan.

—*Sept. 2:* The official ceremony proclaiming the Japanese surrender is held on the deck of the USS *Missouri*.

Chapter 1

This Is No Drill

December 7, 1941, dawned as a routine Sunday morning at Pearl Harbor, Hawaii. On the American military base, some men and women slept late while others attended church services. The distant rumble of aircraft over the Pacific Ocean did not alarm anyone at the army or navy bases at Pearl.

Suddenly, the earth shook and a powerful bomb blast rocked the morning stillness. Sailors and soldiers looked to the sky to see dozens of roaring airplanes. A red circle resembling a blood-red sun, the symbol of Japan, was painted on their wings. The planes flew so low that men on the ground could see the pilots' faces.

Stunned by the surprise of this attack, the Americans were too shocked to fire back at the enemy. Onboard the battleship USS *Nevada*, a crew raised the flag while a Marine band played the national anthem. With no warning a Japanese plane burst out of the clouds and sprayed the *Nevada*'s deck with machine-gun fire. Amazingly, the band completed the anthem without missing a note.

Battleships, laying at anchor in a formation the sailors called "battleship row," were prime targets. Like hawks seeking prey, Japanese torpedo planes swept down upon the USS *Oklahoma*. Torpedoes seared the water, racing toward the side of the great ship. Five torpedoes exploded against the *Oklahoma*, and the battleship rolled over.

Half a dozen dive-bombers screamed toward the USS *Arizona*. At least one bomb crashed through the deck and exploded in an ammunition hold. Though it weighed

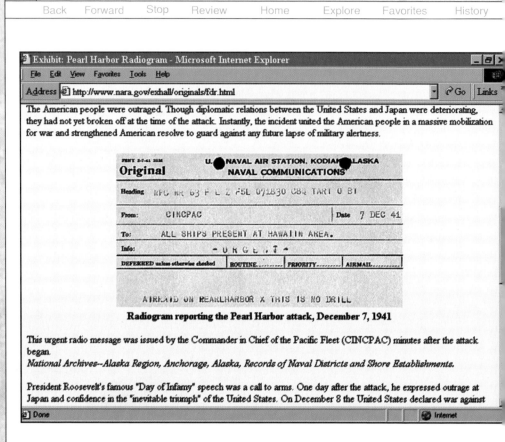

The American people were outraged. Though diplomatic relations between the United States and Japan were deteriorating, they had not yet broken off at the time of the attack. Instantly, the incident united the American people in a massive mobilization for war and strengthened American resolve to guard against any future lapse of military alertness.

Original	U. NAVAL AIR STATION, KODIAK ALASKA NAVAL COMMUNICATIONS	
Heading	RFC NR 63 F L Z F5L 071830 C8U TARI U 81	
From:	CINCPAC	Date 7 DEC 41
To:	ALL SHIPS PRESENT AT HAWAIIN AREA.	
Info:	- URGENT -	
DEFERRED unless otherwise checked	ROUTINE......... PRIORITY......... AIRMAIL.........	

AIRRAID ON REARLHARBOR X THIS IS NO DRILL

Radiogram reporting the Pearl Harbor attack, December 7, 1941

This urgent radio message was issued by the Commander in Chief of the Pacific Fleet (CINCPAC) minutes after the attack began.
National Archives--Alaska Region, Anchorage, Alaska, Records of Naval Districts and Shore Establishments.

President Roosevelt's famous "Day of Infamy" speech was a call to arms. One day after the attack, he expressed outrage at Japan and confidence in the "inevitable triumph" of the United States. On December 8 the United States declared war against

▲ This is the actual radiogram reporting the attack on Pearl Harbor, December 7, 1941.

more than thirty thousand tons, the *Arizona* jumped a foot before bursting into flames and sinking in the shallow harbor waters. Only the top decks, swept with fire, remained above the surface. A navy officer on a nearby ship described the ghastly scene, "[I] could see the men on [the] *Arizona* walking on deck burning alive . . . They were a ghostly crew as they walked out of those flames. And then they just dropped dead."[1]

Minutes after the first bomb fell, a radio operator sent out a message that electrified the world: AIR RAID, PEARL HARBOR—THIS IS NO DRILL.

Home television did not exist in 1941, but soon radios across the nation buzzed with reports of the Japanese "sneak attack." Americans reacted with fury, fear, and deep sadness.

The next day a grim president, Franklin D. Roosevelt, addressed the nation. He called December 7, 1941, "a date which will live in infamy . . . " Roosevelt asked Congress to declare war against Japan. Three days later, Germany and Italy, allies of Japan, declared war on the United States. Pearl Harbor, the "day of infamy," had plunged the United States of America into World War II.

When the smoke cleared at Pearl Harbor, Americans counted their losses. The air assault lasted less than ninety minutes, but killed some 2,400 Americans. More than 1,000 sailors died on the *Arizona* alone. Seven of the eight battleships anchored at Pearl Harbor were sunk or severely damaged.

The horrifying destruction and the underhanded nature of the Japanese attack outraged the American people. After December 7, 1941, Americans united and marched into war with a single battle cry: "Remember Pearl Harbor!"

President Franklin D. ▶
Roosevelt led the
country through most
of World War II.

Chapter 2

Rising Sun

Lines from a song, popular among Japanese soldiers and sailors at the start of World War II, follow:

> Across the sea, corpses in the water;
> Across the mountain, corpses in the field.
> I shall die only for the Emperor,
> I shall never look back.[1]

▶ War Comes to the Pacific

World War II was the most costly war in human history. An estimated 55 million people died as a result of the conflict. Because the war was global, the United States was forced to fight over two oceans—the Atlantic and the Pacific.

How did this terrible clash of arms begin? Officially, World War II broke out in Europe on September 1, 1939, when Germany invaded Poland. However, some historians believe the war actually started in 1931, when the Japanese Army marched into Manchuria. Six years later, in July 1937, Chinese and Japanese troops exchanged shots near an ancient stone bridge named for Marco Polo in the Chinese city of Peking (now Beijing, the capital of China). Japan used this "bridge incident" as an excuse to wage war on China. By late 1938, Japanese Army units occupied large areas of China and most of that country's major port cities.

Warlords rose to power in the early 1930s. These warlords, or regional leaders, controlled the Japanese

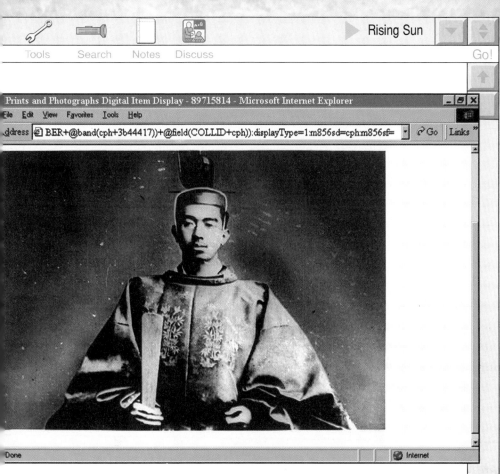

Prints and Photographs Digital Item Display - 89715814 - Microsoft Internet Explorer

File   Edit   View   Favorites   Tools   Help

...ddress ☰ BER+@band(cph+3b44417))+@field(COLLID+cph)):displayType=1:m856sd=cph:m856sf=   ⌐Go   Links "

Done   Internet

▲ *Emperor Hirohito of Japan.*

government. They convinced the Japanese public that the country's survival depended on expansion. Japan was an island nation, poor in resources. Iron ore, rubber, and oil were desperately needed to keep Japan's industries running. At the time many neighboring states, which had plentiful resources, were controlled by European powers. Indonesia, the world's leading source of crude rubber, was a Dutch colony. Malaya, a British colony, was a major tin producer. Japanese leaders raised the cry, "Asia for the Asians." The warlords posed as liberators seeking to free fellow Asians from the yoke of white colonial rule. However, the Japanese leaders also hoped to gain control of China's natural resources for Japan.

The United States government viewed the situation in Asia with alarm, yet it was reluctant to act. Americans were focused on the war in Europe. Still, the United States could not ignore the turmoil in Asia. America had military bases in Hawaii and in other points in the Pacific. The Philippines had been an American colony since 1898.

Hoping to curb Japanese expansion, President Franklin Roosevelt forbade American companies from shipping oil, iron ore, and scrap iron to Japan. This trade embargo enraged the warlords. The Japanese government decided to declare war on the United States and struck a crushing blow on the American fleet at Pearl Harbor.

▶ Masters of the Pacific

The Pearl Harbor attack was the first step in a coordinated Japanese effort to oust Americans and Europeans from the Pacific region. Hours after bombs fell on Pearl Harbor, Japanese airplanes attacked United States outposts in Wake Island, Guam, and the Philippines. Japanese armies stormed the Dutch colony of Indonesia and invaded the Malay Peninsula, a British territory. On December 10, 1941, Japanese bombers sank two of Great Britain's finest warships, HMS *Repulse* and HMS *Prince of Wales*, killing 800 British sailors. It marked the first time airplanes destroyed warships that were sailing on the high seas.

In mid-December 1941, more than 56,000 Japanese troops landed on beaches at Luzon, the major island in the Philippines. Within two weeks, the invaders entered Manila, the capital of the Philippines. American and Filipino troops fell back to the Bataan Peninsula. There they waged a heroic resistance even though they were desperately short of food and ammunition. As the siege of Bataan continued, men were reduced to eating grass and even rats. In early May 1942, some 60,000 American and Filipino soldiers surrendered to the Japanese Army. The captives were marched in blistering heat to camps seventy miles away. About ten thousand of the prisoners died of malaria, starvation, or beatings at the hands of their guards. The terrible ordeal became known as the "Bataan Death March."

In March 1942, President Roosevelt ordered General Douglas MacArthur, the American commander in the Philippines, to escape to Australia. Before MacArthur left his post, he made a statement that became an inspiration for Filipinos and Americans alike: "I shall return."

By June, the Japanese Empire reached its zenith. Burma, Hong Kong, Indonesia, the Solomon and Gilbert Islands, and the Philippines lay under the flag of the rising sun. In all, more than one million square miles of land and 150 million people had been added to the empire.

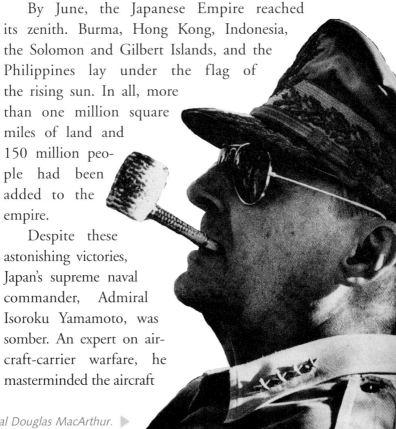

Despite these astonishing victories, Japan's supreme naval commander, Admiral Isoroku Yamamoto, was somber. An expert on aircraft-carrier warfare, he masterminded the aircraft

General Douglas MacArthur. ▶

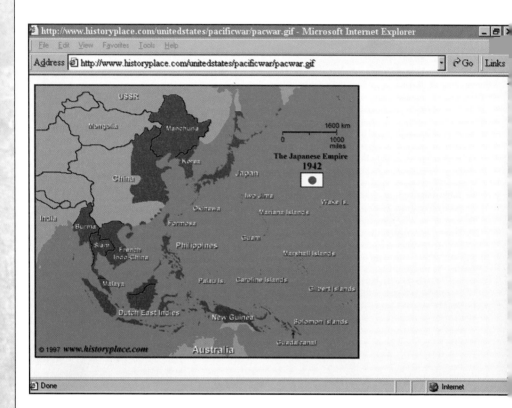

http://www.historyplace.com/unitedstates/pacificwar/pacwar.gif - Microsoft Internet Explorer

File   Edit   View   Favorites   Tools   Help

Address http://www.historyplace.com/unitedstates/pacificwar/pacwar.gif   Go   Links

Done   Internet

▲ The Japanese Empire had reached its greatest size in 1942.

carrier strike that devastated Pearl Harbor. He hoped striking a savage first blow would force America and her allies to seek peace. A long war, he feared, would doom Japan. Yamamoto expressed his views directly. "In the first six to twelve months of a war with the United States and Great Britain, I will run wild and win victory after victory. After that . . . I have no expectation of success."[2] After Pearl Harbor, Yamamoto cautioned other Japanese commanders. "I fear that all we have done is awakened a sleeping giant, and filled him with a terrible resolve."[3] Yamamoto keenly understood that the might of the American fleet was still intact, because not all their carriers were destroyed during the attack on Pearl Harbor.

Chapter 3

The Tide Turns

On April 18, 1942, a B-25 bomber slowly, almost painfully, lifted from the deck of the USS *Hornet*. The B-25 was a two-engine, land-based plane that was not meant to operate from the tiny deck of an aircraft carrier. Yet sixteen of these giants, led by Lieutenant Colonel James H. Doolittle, managed to lumber off the *Hornet* and proceed to Japan. After flying almost four hours, the B-25s struck their targets in Japan and then crash-landed in China. The bombs did little damage, but the daring raid cheered up Americans at home, weary after a dismal string of defeats. Doolittle and his men became instant heroes.

In May 1942, a Japanese and an American carrier fleet clashed in the Coral Sea near New Guinea. The Battle of the Coral Sea was the first of its kind in the history of naval warfare. The two fleets never came within 100 miles of each other. After four days of combat, the Japanese had lost one of their carriers. The United States suffered the loss of the USS *Lexington*.

▶ Midway, the Turning Point in the Pacific

Early in June 1942, a small Japanese carrier force attacked the Aleutians, the chain of islands that trails away from Alaska. The attack served as a lure, part of a clever plan created by Admiral Yamamoto. The admiral hoped to draw American warships farther north. Then Yamamoto intended to land a large force on Midway, a small island, about 1,200 miles west of Hawaii. The landing would

bring the American fleet into the open seas where it could be destroyed in one climactic battle.

Unknown to Yamamoto, his plan was almost an open book to his foe. American experts had cracked the complicated Japanese military code months earlier. When Yamamoto launched his diversionary attack on the Aleutians, the American commander, Admiral Chester Nimitz, refused to swallow the bait. Thanks to the skill of the codebreakers, Nimitz concentrated his forces at Midway Island. Nimitz knew the main Japanese fleet sailed in these waters.

At first, the two navies probed at each other like boxers in a ring. Airplanes engaged in vicious dogfights, but

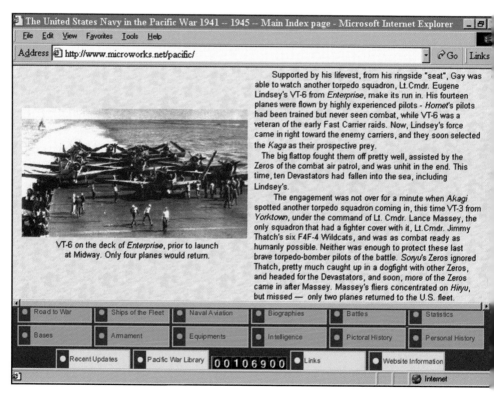

The United States Navy in the Pacific War 1941 -- 1945 -- Main Index page - Microsoft Internet Explorer

File   Edit   View   Favorites   Tools   Help

Address http://www.microworks.net/pacific/   Go   Links

Supported by his lifevest, from his ringside "seat", Gay was able to watch another torpedo squadron, Lt.Cmdr. Eugene Lindsey's VT-6 from *Enterprise*, make its run in. His fourteen planes were flown by highly experienced pilots - *Hornet*'s pilots had been trained but never seen combat, while VT-6 was a veteran of the early Fast Carrier raids. Now, Lindsey's force came in right toward the enemy carriers, and they soon selected the *Kaga* as their prospective prey.

The big flattop fought them off pretty well, assisted by the Zeros of the combat air patrol, and was unhit in the end. This time, ten Devastators had fallen into the sea, including Lindsey's.

The engagement was not over for a minute when *Akagi* spotted another torpedo squadron coming in, this time VT-3 from *Yorktown*, under the command of Lt. Cmdr. Lance Massey, the only squadron that had a fighter cover with it, Lt.Cmdr. Jimmy Thatch's six F4F-4 Wildcats, and was as combat ready as humanly possible. Neither was enough to protect these last brave torpedo-bomber pilots of the battle. *Soryu*'s Zeros ignored Thatch, pretty much caught up in a dogfight with other Zeros, and headed for the Devastators, and soon, more of the Zeros came in after Massey. Massey's fliers concentrated on *Hiryu*, but missed — only two planes returned to the U.S. fleet.

VT-6 on the deck of *Enterprise*, prior to launch at Midway. Only four planes would return.

Road to War | Ships of the Fleet | Naval Aviation | Biographies | Battles | Statistics

Bases | Armament | Equipments | Intelligence | Pictoral History | Personal History

Recent Updates | Pacific War Library   00106900   Links | Website Information

Internet

▲ *Only four of these planes would return from the Battle of Midway.*

neither side struck a decisive blow. On June 4, 1942, Japanese carrier planes bombed bases on Midway Island. Japanese commanders reasoned that their bombers had not done sufficient damage to the island, so they readied the planes for a second strike. Suddenly, American dive-bombers zoomed out of the sky. The Japanese carriers' decks were crisscrossed with gasoline hoses and strewn with bombs ready to be loaded onto Japanese planes. The Americans had caught the enemy ships in a most vulnerable state. American bombs tore into decks, and the huge carriers erupted into sheets of flame. In just five breathtaking minutes, the Japanese fleet lost three of its finest aircraft carriers.

Mitsuo Fuchida, a Japanese officer serving on the aircraft carrier *Akagi*, which sunk at Midway, recalled this horrific incident. "The terrifying scream of the dive bombers reached me first, followed by the crashing of a direct hit. There was a blinding flash and then a second explosion much louder than the first."[1]

The tremendous sea battle lasted forty-eight hours. Four Japanese aircraft carriers were sunk, and the Americans lost the carrier USS *Yorktown*. Both sides suffered terrible losses, but clearly the Japanese emerged as the defeated party. More than 3,500 Japanese sailors perished and 275 of their best airplanes were destroyed. Midway was a blow from which the Japanese never recovered. After this battle, Japan never again launched another major offensive naval operation.

Guadalcanal, the Hellish Island

On August 7, 1942, some eleven thousand U.S. Marines came ashore on the jungle-covered island of Guadalcanal. Here the Japanese were building an airfield, which they

hoped to use as a base from which to strike Australia. The Americans caught their foe completely by surprise. Marines captured the still incomplete airfield in less than twenty-four hours. The only casualty occurred when a young Marine cut his hand while opening a coconut with a bayonet.

The Marines quickly discovered Guadalcanal was a hellish place. Land crabs, looking like creatures out of a nightmare, crawled on the ground. Spiders the size of golf balls hung in the trees. Swarms of flies flew so thick the men could not eat a forkful of food without swallowing at least one of the insects. Mosquitoes tormented the Marines night and day.

▲ *Marines landing on Guadalcanal Island, where they would find themselves subject to malaria, huge spiders and crabs, and relentless insects. The Guadalcanal campaign would prove to be one of the most difficult of World War II.*

Soon the enemy struck back. On a pitch dark night, forty-eight hours after the landings, a force of Japanese warships approached the American and Australian ships patrolling near the island. Big guns roared and the night blazed with orange shell bursts and searchlight beams. In forty minutes, four Allied heavy cruisers were sunk and more than a thousand American and Australian sailors were killed. Hundreds more were wounded, burned, or struggling to avoid death in those shark-infested waters. Not one Japanese ship was hit. It was one of the greatest Japanese naval victories of the war.

Night after night, Japanese warships returned to pound the U.S. Marines on land with their heavy guns. Furious land battles broke out between Japanese soldiers and the Marines. On a rain-swept night in September 1942, waves of Japanese soldiers, shouting "Banzai!" (translated "Long Live the Emperor"), rushed the Marines dug in on a ridge near the airfield. In the grisly encounter, the Marines fought with artillery fire, machine guns, hand grenades, and finally with bayonets. At sunrise, the mangled and twisted bodies of some six hundred Japanese soldiers lay on the ridge.

For six months, American forces built a stronghold on Guadalcanal. Gradually Japanese attacks diminished. Malaria, a disease spread by the ever-present mosquitoes, killed more Americans than did Japanese fire. In all, more than four thousand Americans lost their lives during the Guadalcanal campaign. Guadalcanal was a grim beginning to the land war in the Pacific. It was a conflict in which young men were ordered to bleed and die on dismal islands they had never heard of before and whose names they could barely pronounce.

Chapter 4 ▶

The War at Home

Pearl Harbor triggered nationwide hatred against Japan and against Japanese people. This hatred released an energy that drove Americans at home to work harder in shipyards and factories. Unfortunately, a revenge-seeking country also turned on its own citizens.

▶ Japanese Internment

"Personally I hate the Japanese, and that goes for all of them . . . Herd 'em up, pack 'em off, and give them the inside room in the badlands,"[1] so wrote Westbrook Pegler, a popular newspaper reporter, on January 29, 1942. Millions of ordinary men and women echoed Pegler's views around the country. Japanese residents in California were refused service in restaurants and grocery stores. They were even turned away from churches.

Complicating this bitterness was a fear of enemy activity along the country's Pacific coast. Early in the war, some Californians lived in fear of Japanese spies, saboteurs, or even an invading army. Wild rumors fueled such fears. Japanese fishermen living in California were suspected of owning radios capable of receiving broadcasts from Tokyo. Another story claimed a Japanese gardener cut his grass in the form of an arrow aimed at a power plant in order to aid enemy bombers. In fact, there was no hard evidence suggesting any Japanese Americans were disloyal. The facts simply got lost or ignored in the panic generated by wartime frustration and anger.

In February 1942, President Roosevelt signed Executive Order 9066. The order forcibly moved Japanese Americans from the West Coast states of California, Oregon, and Washington. Within weeks some 112,000 men, women, and children were relocated to barbed wire enclosed camps. Isolated and scorned, some of the camp inmates collapsed under the strain. A teenager named Ben Tagami wrote, "Mom went through hell. She finally cracked and had a nervous breakdown . . . [She] cried all day, all night."[2]

Despite their deplorable environment, camp residents led a somewhat dignified life. They formed schools and

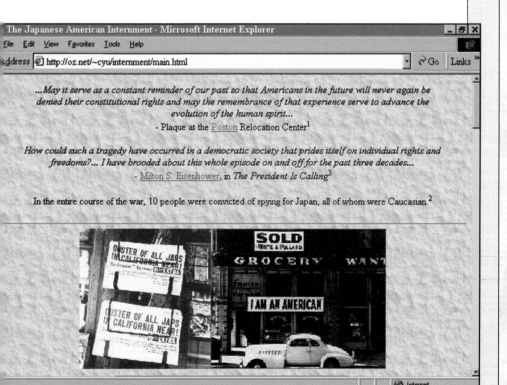

The Japanese American Internment - Microsoft Internet Explorer

File   Edit   View   Favorites   Tools   Help

Address http://oz.net/~cyu/internment/main.html   Go   Links

...May it serve as a constant reminder of our past so that Americans in the future will never again be denied their constitutional rights and may the remembrance of that experience serve to advance the evolution of the human spirit...
- Plaque at the Poston Relocation Center[1]

How could such a tragedy have occurred in a democratic society that prides itself on individual rights and freedoms?... I have brooded about this whole episode on and off for the past three decades...
- Milton S. Eisenhower, in *The President Is Calling*[3]

In the entire course of the war, 10 people were convicted of spying for Japan, all of whom were Caucasian.[2]

Internet

▲ A Japanese storekeeper hangs a banner in front of his store that shows his patriotism. Despite the loyalty they showed to the United States, many Japanese Americans were confined to internment camps.

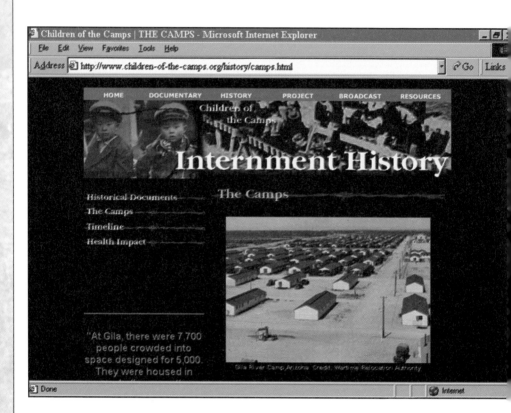

Children of the Camps | THE CAMPS - Microsoft Internet Explorer

File Edit View Favorites Tools Help

Address http://www.children-of-the-camps.org/history/camps.html   Go   Links

HOME   DOCUMENTARY   HISTORY   PROJECT   BROADCAST   RESOURCES

Children of
the Camps

Internment History

Historical Documents
The Camps
Timeline
Health Impact

The Camps

"At Gila, there were 7,700
people crowded into
space designed for 5,000.
They were housed in

Gila River Camp, Arizona. Credit, Wartime Relocation Authority

Done   Internet

▲ More than 120,000 Japanese Americans were incarcerated in internment camps in the western United States during World War II.

Boy and Girl Scout troops. To the amazement of their guards, inmates began their day by raising the American flag and reciting the Pledge of Allegiance. Yet none would ever forget the anger they felt at being secluded and locked up simply because of their ethnic heritage. In a 1944 case, Supreme Court Justice Frank Murphy asserted that the internment program was a "legalization of racism."[3] Constitutional scholar Edward Corwin called the internment of Japanese Americans "the most dramatic invasion of the rights [of United States citizens] by their own government that had thus far occurred in the history of our nation."[4]

▶ Revolution in the Ship Yards

The Pacific Ocean covers more than one-third of the earth's surface. To fight a war on this expanse requires an enormous fleet of ships. Fueled by the pressures of war, American ship production reached miraculous levels. In less than four years, American workers turned out more vessels than every other country in the world had before the war.

The United States started the war with only five aircraft carriers. By war's end shipyards had assembled seventeen huge 35,000-ton *Essex*-class carrier ships. Cargo vessels were essential to transport goods. The workhorse of American cargo carriers was the *Liberty*, a clumsy-looking vessel about half the length of a football field. Workers on

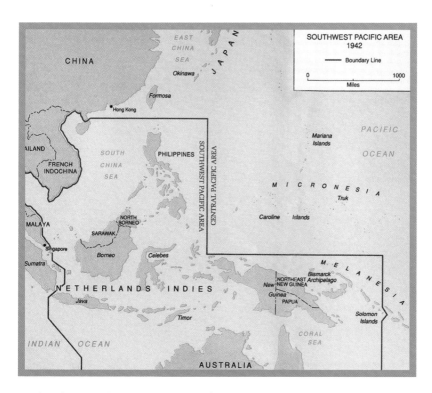

▲ The map shows the South Pacific area.

both coasts toiled night and day, reducing the assembly time of a *Liberty* from one hundred days to forty days.

As more and more men were drafted into the army, women took on the heavy work in shipyards. Initially, old-time shipbuilders believed women were too dainty to handle the rugged workload. Women quickly proved their critics wrong. More than one-third of the work force was female in many shipyards.

Factories producing war goods, such as tanks and trucks, also had a huge female workforce. "Rosie the Riveter," pictured as a muscular, but pretty, young lady dressed in coveralls, became the symbol of industrial America. Though women achieved gains in the workplace, they also suffered loneliness and anxiety. Women on the home front knew their husbands, brothers, sweethearts, and sons were in constant danger in war zones. It is no wonder that songs popular with women during wartime often had a sad, wait-for-me theme:

> I'll be with you in apple blossom time.
> I'll be with you to change your name to mine.[5]

Bloody Path to Japan

The Pacific Ocean is studded with hundreds of islands. To American generals and admirals, those islands were rungs on a ladder that led to Japan. The Japanese viewed the islands as fortresses whose defenders were willing— and seemingly eager—to fight until death. William Manchester, a Marine who later became a journalist, wrote of his experience in this Pacific War: "Somebody . . . said that war was a game of inches, like baseball; the width of your thumb could determine whether you were killed, wounded, or completely spared."[1]

▶ The Island Campaign

Tarawa's central island covered 291 acres, making it just slightly larger than the average farm in the United States. In November 1943, some five thousand American Marines invaded this tiny island. First to approach the beach were waves of amphibious tractors (fighting vehicles) called amtracs. While still in the water, artillery shells and rifle fire poured onto the amtracs, sinking them and setting them ablaze. Next came the flat-bottomed Higgins boats, each crowded with up to fifty Marines. The boats bumped into the coral reef ringing the island. Marines aboard were forced to wade ashore in chest-deep water while machine-gun bullets rained down upon them. The battle for Tarawa lasted less than three days, but resulted in 1,000 Americans dead and twice that number wounded. Such was the nature of the island fighting in the Pacific War.

Prints and Photographs Digital Item Display - 96507004 - Microsoft Internet Explorer

File   Edit   View   Favorites   Tools   Help

Address BER+@band(cph+3b38742))+@field(COLLID+cph)):displayType=1:m856sd=cph:m856sf=   Go   Links

Done   Internet

▲ *A Japanese soldier.*

More island battles followed: Kwajalein, Eniwetok, Saipan, Peleliu, and places so small and so remote they went unmentioned in geography books. Naval leaders often bypassed certain Japanese island strong points and surrounded them with ships instead of invading the shores.

Though both U.S. Army and Marine troops participated in island operations, the Marine Corps was specially trained for amphibious warfare. The typical Marine was youthful. He was also proud to serve in what he considered the nation's elite branch of service. Still, savage island fighting wore out even the most energetic soldiers. E. B. Sledge, a Marine on Peleliu, recalled "The grinding stress of prolonged heavy combat, the loss of sleep . . . the

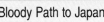
unrelenting, suffocating heat were enough to make us drop in our tracks . . . I became fatalistic, praying only for my [death] to be painless."[2]

The Silent Service

While the fleet lay in ruins at Pearl Harbor, American submarines ventured into the Pacific to sink enemy vessels. For the first two years of the war, the underwater boats were rendered ineffective by faulty torpedoes. Lack of testing was the major problem. Before Pearl Harbor, naval officers were reluctant to waste their very expensive torpedoes on practice targets. As a result, defective firing devices went unnoticed. By late 1943, the firing problem was

This map shows the Central Pacific, where soldiers fought battles on remote tiny islands.

fixed, and United States submarines launched deadly offensive operations deep inside Japanese-held waters.

By war's end, the American submarine fleet had sunk more than 1,100 Japanese cargo-carrying ships. In effect, the submarines choked Japan, reducing its shipping to a fraction of the raw material the nation needed to carry out the war. In November 1944, the submarine USS *Archerfish* brought down the huge Japanese carrier *Shinano*, marking the greatest single submarine victory of the war.

The submarine force was called the "silent service" because its missions were shrouded in secrecy. When an American submarine was sunk, the U.S. Navy refused to publicize the loss, so as not to inform the enemy of its success. The silent service contributed mightily to America's victory but at a terrible cost. During the course of the war, fifty-two submarines went down with a loss of 3,505 American sailors.

▶ MacArthur Returns

On October 20, 1944, General Douglas MacArthur stepped off a landing craft and waded ashore at Leyte, a large island in the center of the Philippines. "People of the Philippines, I have returned,"[3] MacArthur announced. From Leyte, the American Army began a bitter four-month struggle to subdue Japanese resistance on Philippine soil.

As the offensive began, the Japanese threw their remaining ships into one last, desperate clash with the U.S. Navy. The Battle of Leyte Gulf lasted from October 23 to October 26, 1944. In terms of ship tonnage involved, Leyte Gulf was the biggest episode of naval warfare in world history. The Japanese fleet was obliterated after three days of fierce combat. Four Japanese carriers, three battleships, nine cruisers, and eight destroyers were sunk. An estimated ten thousand Japanese seamen lost their lives.

During the height of the Leyte battle, a lone Japanese plane dove toward the USS *Santee*, an escort carrier. American ships sent up a hail of antiaircraft fire, yet the determined Japanese pilot kept his craft on a steady line toward the carrier. As sailors on neighboring ships watched in horrifying fascination, the plane crashed into the *Santee* and exploded in a ball of fire. This was the American Navy's first clash with a kamikaze; a Japanese suicide bomber. In the near future, kamikazes would terrorize the skies over the Pacific.

The American Experience | MacArthur | Maps | WWII: The battle for Leyte - Microsoft Internet Explorer

File   Edit   View   Favorites   Tools   Help

Address http://www.pbs.org/wgbh/amex/macarthur/maps/leyte01.html   Go   Links

WWII: The Battle for Leyte   (1 of 4)

One of the most memorable images of World War II is that of MacArthur wading ashore at Leyte, making good on his pledge to return to and liberate his beloved Philippines. But often lost in the story is the epic battle being waged around him, which included the greatest naval engagement in history and a long, difficult land campaign.

As both prongs of the Allied advance -- MacArthur's and Nimitz's -- gained speed in 1944, the Japanese grew determined to make a stand in the Philippines. Most American war planners expected greatest resistance in Luzon, where Japanese air bases in

MacArthur's operations leading up to Leyte
MacArthur's operations after Leyte
Nimitz's operations leading up to Leyte

Done   Internet

▲ This map shows the Battle for Leyte campaign, one of the biggest episodes of naval warfare in world history. It lasted from October 23 to October 26, 1944.

Japan's Last Stand

In mid-1944, a new airplane—the B-29 bomber—began to roll off production lines in the United States. Sleek and powerful, the four-engine giant was the biggest combat aircraft employed in World War II. The B-29 carried ten tons of bombs, flew at a rate of 365 miles an hour, and had a range of almost 6,000 miles. These planes brought the war to the Japanese homeland.

B-29s took off from airfields built on the newly won islands of Tinian and Saipan, about 1,600 miles from Tokyo. However, these air raids did not achieve their targets. Bomber commander General Curtis LeMay determined the B-29s flew too high to accurately hit factories and railroad yards. So LeMay ordered the bombers to come in low and drop thousands of incendiary bombs on Japanese cities. Incendiary bombs were designed to start raging fires, spreading eventually to vital industrial areas.

On the night of March 10, 1945, a fleet of 325 B-29s swept over Tokyo, dropping hundreds of incendiary bombs. Soon the city was engulfed in a hurricane of flames. One woman remembered trying to flee from the town with her family while the fires pursued them, "like a wild animal."[1] Estimates vary, but at least eighty-three thousand Tokyo residents lost their lives in that one air raid.

In the course of the war, B-29s dropped firebombs on sixty-six cities. Most of these raids took place at night. Wartime Japanese cities were crowded with factory workers. Houses were made up mostly of paper and wood.

These incendiary attacks killed at least half a million people and reduced entire neighborhoods to ashes. Survivors of the raids were left homeless and shaken, and many had terrible burns covering their bodies.

▶ Uncommon Valor

From the sea, the island of Iwo Jima looked like a worthless rock dominated by the cone-shaped mountain called Suribachi. Yet this desolate spot was valuable real estate. It contained an airfield where fighter planes could take off and accompany the B-29s to their targets. Also, crippled bombers could land there.

▲ *The island of Iwo Jima was a strategic place where fighter planes could land and take off. After a brutal struggle and thousands of dead and wounded, the Americans captured the island.*

▲ The flag raising on Mount Suribachi, Iwo Jima, taken by Joe
Rosenthal, is perhaps the most famous photograph of World War II.

For seventy-three days, attack aircraft and the heavy
guns of ships bombarded Iwo Jima. On February 19,
1945, the Marines hit the beach. Despite the prolonged
bombardment, hundreds of Japanese artillery pieces sur-
vived and advancing Marines were fired upon from hidden
caves. Every inch of this black sandy island beach was a target. There was no respite, no secure place behind the lines
to treat the wounded or to lay the dead. Twisted bodies of
young Marines covered the landing areas.

The battle raged for thirty days. The Marines lost
6,000 dead and 25,000 suffered wounds. One in every
three Americans that took part in the struggle for Iwo Jima
became a casualty. The Japanese, as was their custom,
fought till the death. Only 216 defenders were taken alive,
and those were either badly wounded or driven insane
from the furious combat.

From the carnage of Iwo Jima came the most famous photograph of World War II. Four days after the landings, a photographer named Joe Rosenthal snapped what he thought was a routine picture of a group of Marines raising the American flag over Mt. Suribachi. The picture thrilled war-weary Americans at home. Today the scene is enshrined in the U.S. Marine Corps Memorial that stands outside Washington, D.C. Under the huge statue are words describing Marine heroism at Iwo Jima: UNCOMMON VALOR WAS A COMMON VIRTUE.

▶ Ordeal at Okinawa

On April 1, 1945, a force of 60,000 men invaded Okinawa, a large island just 450 miles from mainland Japan. It was Easter Sunday, normally a day of peace and prayer. To everyone's amazement the landings were easy. Soldiers and Marines marched inland instead of having to fight their way off the beaches. Then, when they reached the south end of the island, the Americans met the bulk of the Japanese defenders. Here the bloodiest series of battles in the Pacific War broke out.

At sea, an armada of 1,500 American ships, the most powerful fleet ever assembled in the Pacific, ringed Okinawa. This was an inviting target for Japanese suicide bombers. Kamikaze means "divine wind." The concept has deep roots in Japanese history. In the year 1281, a Mongol invasion fleet heading for Japan was sunk by a violent wind, which the Japanese people believed was sent by God. Now, once more, the nation was to be saved by a new divine wind. Like human-driven guided missiles, the kamikazes crashed on more than three hundred American ships from April to June 1945. Thirty-six ships were sunk,

bar

and almost five thousand American sailors perished in the bloodiest engagement in U.S. naval history.

Germany surrendered on May 7, 1945, but that development on the other side of the world meant little to the defenders of Okinawa. Japanese resistance continued until mid-June 1945. By then more than 49,000 Americans had been killed or wounded. The Japanese lost an estimated 109,000 men, and about 75,000 Okinawan civilians were killed. William Manchester expressed his first-hand account of the experience: "There was so much death [on Okinawa] that life seemed almost indecent. Some men's uniforms were soaked with gobs of blood. The ground was sodden with it."[2]

▲ *Major General Lemuel C. Shepherd studying a map of Okinawa.*

The Price of Peace

While vacationing in Warm Springs, Georgia, President Franklin Roosevelt complained of having a headache. Shortly after, he collapsed and died. The date was April 12, 1945. The American people mourned the man who had been their commander in chief for more than twelve years. Roosevelt's sudden death propelled little-known Vice President Harry Truman to the nation's highest office. Following his swearing in, Truman was informed that the nation was developing a revolutionary and frighteningly powerful nuclear weapon.

Three months later, in the desert of New Mexico, a group of scientists crouched in concrete bunkers. All wore dark glasses. It was early morning July 16, 1945, and the men awaited the first test firing of the atomic bomb. After a tense countdown the earth shook, a terrible roar ripped the desert stillness, and a brilliant flash filled the darkened sky. Robert Oppenheimer, one of the scientists who helped to build the nuclear device, was deeply moved by what he saw. From the Bhagavad Gita, a sacred poem, he remembered these words, "I am become Death, the shatterer of worlds."[1]

Harry Truman became ▶ president when Roosevelt died on April 12, 1945.

The Atomic Bomb

The atomic bomb was created in a super-secret effort called the Manhattan Project. More than 100,000 people worked on the undertaking, yet only a handful knew they were building an atomic bomb. Manhattan Project engineers spent about $2 billion of scarce wartime funds. Now the bomb was ready and in the hands of an untried leader, Harry Truman.

President Truman faced an agonizing decision: Should he order this devastating bomb to be dropped on Japan, a nation so close to defeat? Many Manhattan Project scientists urged him not to employ the weapon because it would cause an unimaginable number of civilian deaths. No doubt Truman thought of the diehard Japanese resistance on Iwo Jima and Okinawa. An assault on the enemy homeland now loomed as the most ghastly battle imaginable in what was already a horrendous war. In Japan stood a 3 million-man army, nine thousand planes, which could be used as kamikazes, and a civilian population determined to fight till death. American military leaders claimed that as many as half a million Americans could die in a land invasion of Japan. After pondering the alternatives, Truman issued orders to use the atomic bomb.

Hiroshima and Nagasaki

On August 6, 1945, a B-29, the *Enola Gay*, approached the city of Hiroshima, Japan. At 8:15 A.M., it dropped its single bomb. On city streets below, men and women hurried to their jobs and children hustled off to school. Suddenly, a ball of fire infinitely brighter than the sun burst above them. Those directly under the blast were incinerated. Trucks and cars were tossed about as if they were toys.

▲ A portion of the Enola Gay, the plane that dropped the bomb on Hiroshima, Japan.

An estimated eighty thousand people died in Hiroshima on the first day, and many more perished later of radiation sickness caused by the bomb.

After Hiroshima, events in the Pacific War moved at a breathtaking pace. On August 8, The Soviet Union declared war on Japan, and the very next day the United States dropped another atomic bomb on the city of Nagasaki. President Truman warned Japanese leaders must surrender or, " . . . they may expect a rain of ruin from the air, the like of which has never been seen on this earth."[2] On August 14, Tokyo agreed to surrender terms. On September 2, the official surrender ceremony was

held aboard the USS *Missouri*, a battleship anchored in Tokyo Bay.

Finally the horrible conflict was over. After forty-five months of warfare, the United States was once again at peace. People rushed to be with family and friends, to embrace each other and to celebrate this special moment. Church bells pealed. Motorists honked their car horns. People flooded the streets of the big cities. Confetti filled the air like snow in downtown New York City. Perfect strangers hugged and kissed. This awful war had ended.

▶ The Aftermath

From the outset of the war, America and its allies demanded Japan's unconditional surrender. In the end, the Allies granted one concession: The Japanese were

allowed to keep their emperor. This proved to be a wise decision. Retaining Emperor Hirohito as a figurehead gave stability to postwar Japan. In a message broadcast on August 14, 1945, Hirohito urged the Japanese people to "Bear the unbearable . . . " Upon surrender, American forces occupied Japan. General Douglas MacArthur headed Japan's postwar government. The nation became a

◀ *The second atomic bomb was dropped on Nagasaki, Japan, on August 9, 1945.*

The New York Times.

JAPAN SURRENDERS, END OF WAR!
EMPEROR ACCEPTS ALLIED RULE;
M'ARTHUR SUPREME COMMANDER;
OUR MANPOWER CURBS VOIDED

▲ This headline from the August 14, 1945, issue of the New York Times declares the end of the war.

democracy under American leadership. Every Japanese citizen gained the right to vote. Labor unions were permitted to organize workers and large estates were broken up to give land to small farmers. Japanese women were granted job opportunities and allowed to participate in government, a truly revolutionary move. When told Japanese men would resent this development, MacArthur said, "I don't care. I want to discredit the military. Women don't want war."[3]

Peace in the Pacific came at a great price. Still, Japan's defeat ended World War II, the costliest war in human experience. General MacArthur spoke for all nations when he signed the peace agreements and said, "Today the guns

are silent. A great tragedy has ended."[4] In a surprisingly short time, Japan and the United States—bitter enemies in war—became close friends in peace.

▶ The Cold War

An all too short peace followed World War II. Then the world drifted into a period known as the Cold War—a sometimes fierce and deadly competition between Communist and non-Communist nations. Asia became caught in the grips of Cold War politics that dominated the postwar world. China became a Communist country in 1949, further altering the political map of Asia. Looming above all was the atomic bomb. The Soviet Union developed its own atomic bomb in 1949. At the end of World War II, the Soviet Union, the world's leading Communist power, occupied the northern portion of Korea while the United States held sway over the southern half of that nation. This situation set the stage for the Korean War, which raged from 1950 to 1953.

The Cold War drew the world into a frightening atomic era. Now humanity faced the prospect of conflict more destructive than any experienced in the past.

Chapter 1. This Is No Drill

1. Gordon Prange, *December 7, 1941: The Day the Japanese Attacked Pearl Harbor* (New York: McGraw-Hill, 1988), p. 145.

Chapter 2. Rising Sun

1. John Toland, *The Rising Sun: The Decline and Fall of the Japanese Empire* (New York: Random House, 1970), vol. 1, p. 287.

2. Arthur Zich, *The Rising Sun* (Alexandria, Va.: Time-Life Books, 1977), p. 19.

3. Isoroku Yamamoto, as quoted by Richard Poe, ed., "Beware the Sleeping Giant," *Frontpage Magazine,* December 7, 2001, <http://www.frontpage.com/poesnotepad/2001/pn12-07-01.htm> (March 8, 2002).

Chapter 3. The Tide Turns

1. John Costello, *The Pacific War* (New York: Rawson, Wade Publishers, Inc., 1981), p. 296.

Chapter 4. The War at Home

1. William Manchester, *The Glory and the Dream* (Boston: Little, Brown and Company, 1974), vol. 1, p. 364.

2. Ellen Levine, *A Fence Away From Freedom* (New York: G. P. Putnam's Sons, 1995), p. 63.

3. Ibid., p. 237.

4. John Whiteclay Chambers, ed. *The Oxford Companion to American Military History* (New York: Oxford Press, 1999), p. 339.

5. Lyrics by Neville Fleeson.

Chapter 5. Bloody Path to Japan

1. William Manchester, *Goodbye, Darkness: A Memoir of the Pacific War* (Boston: Little, Brown and Company, 1980), p. 293.

E. B. Sledge, *With the Old Breed at Peleliu and Okinawa* (New York: Oxford University Press, 1981), p. 147.

3. John Costello, *The Pacific War* (New York: Rawson, Wade Publishers, Inc., 1981), p. 503.

Chapter 6. Japan's Last Stand

1. John Toland, *The Rising Sun: The Decline and Fall of the Japanese Empire* (New York: Random House, 1970), vol. 2, p. 836.

2. William Manchester, *Goodbye, Darkness: A Memoir of the Pacific War* (Boston: Little, Brown and Company, 1980), p. 380.

Chapter 7. The Price of Peace

1. William Manchester, *The Glory and the Dream* (Boston: Little, Brown and Company, 1974), p. 462.

2. John Costello, *The Pacific War* (New York: Rawson, Wade Publishers, Inc., 1981), p. 592.

3. John Toland, *The Rising Sun: The Decline and Fall of the Japanese Empire* (New York: Random House, 1970), vol. 2, p. 1,070.

4. *The Annals of America.* (Chicago: Encyclopedia Britannica, Inc., 1976), vol. 16, p. 339.

Further Reading

Costello, John. *The Pacific War.* New York: Rawson, Wade Publishers, Inc., 1981.

Gonzales, Doreen. *The Manhattan Project and the Atomic Bomb in American History.* Berkeley Heights, N.J.: Enslow Publishers, Inc., 2000.

Grant, R. G. *Hiroshima & Nagasaki.* Orlando, Fla.: Raintree Steck-Vaughn Publishers, 1998.

Levine, Ellen. *A Fence Away From Freedom.* New York: G. P. Putnam's Sons, 1995.

Manchester, William. *The Glory and the Dream.* Boston: Little, Brown and Company, 1974.

————. Goodbye, Darkness: *A Memoir of the Pacific War.* Boston: Little, Brown and Company, 1980.

McGowen, Tom. *Midway & Guadalcanal.* Danbury, Conn.: Watts, Franklin Inc., 1984.

Nardo, Don, *World War II: The War in the Pacific.* San Diego, Calif.: Lucent Books, 1991.

O'Neal, Michael. *President Truman & the Atomic Bomb.* San Diego, Calif.: Greenhaven Press, 1990.

Prange, Gordon. *December 7, 1941: The Day the Japanese Attacked Pearl Harbor.* New York: McGraw-Hill, 1988.

Shapiro, William E. *Pearl Harbor.* Danbury, Conn.: Watts, Franklin Inc., 1984.

Sledge, E. B. *With the Old Breed at Peleliu and Okinawa.* New York: Oxford University Press, 1981.

Stein, R. Conrad. *Battle of Okinawa.* Danbury, Conn.: Children's Press, 1985.

————. *World War II in the Pacific: "Remember Pearl Harbor."* Berkeley Heights, N.J.: Enslow Publishers, Inc., 1994.